W9-CEB-947

HIGH-RISE
WINDOW WASHER:
12 THINGS TO KNOW

by Samantha S. Bell

STORY LIBRARY
MORE TO EXPLORE

www.12StoryLibrary.com

12-Story Library is an imprint of Bookstaves.

Developed and produced for 12-Story Library by Focus Strategic Communications Inc.

Library of Congress Cataloging-in-Publication Data
Names: Bell, Samantha, author.
Title: High-rise window washer : 12 things to know / Samantha S. Bell.
Description: Mankato : 12-Story Library, 2022. | Series: Daring and dangerous jobs | Includes bibliographical references and index. | Audience: Ages 10–12 | Audience: Grades 4–6
Identifiers: LCCN 2020029612 (print) | LCCN 2020029613 (ebook) | ISBN 9781632359407 (library binding) | ISBN 9781632359759 (paperback) | ISBN 9781645821052 (pdf)
Subjects: LCSH: Hazardous occupations—United States—Juvenile literature. | Window cleaners (Persons)—United States—Juvenile literature. | Skyscrapers—United States—Juvenile literature.
Classification: LCC HD7262.5.U6 B45 2022 (print) | LCC HD7262.5.U6 (ebook) | DDC 648.5—dc23
LC record available at https://lccn.loc.gov/2020029612
LC ebook record available at https://lccn.loc.gov/2020029613

Photographs ©: BABAROGA/Shutterstock.com, cover, 1; Science History Images/Alamy, 4; GALA Images ARCHIVE/Alamy, 4; PD, 5; Brian A Jackson/Shutterstock.com, 5; Michael Vi/Shutterstock.com, 6; Edmonton Sun/YouTube.com, 7; Tomasz Czajkowski/Shutterstock.com, 7; EB Adventure Photography/Shutterstock.com, 8; EyeEm/Alamy, 9; AGAMI Photo Agency/Alamy, 9; ilovephoto_KA/Shutterstock.com, 10; Christopher Penler/Shutterstock.com, 11; OldYorkGuy/CC3.0, 11; Katharine Andriotis/Alamy, 12; Edgar Bullon/Alamy, 12; 1010 Wins/YouTube.com, 13; Squeegeeguy #1/YouTube.com, 14, 15; Ronald Hudson/Alamy, 16; PavleMarjanovic/Shutterstock.com, 17; NeydtStock/Shutterstock.com, 17; Window cleaning videos/YouTube.com, 18; On the Spot Window Cleaning/YouTube.com, 19; Tetra Images/Alamy, 20; ElenaR/Shutterstock.com, 20; CANTV/YouTube.com, 21; John Kershner/Shutterstock.com, 21; Westend61 GmbH/Alamy, 21; Patti McConville/Stockimo/Alamy, 22; RGtimeline/Alamy, 22; Valerii Soloviov/Alamy, 23; Dundee Photographics/Alamy, 23; Rocky Grimes/Shutterstock.com, 24; meunierd/Shutterstock.com, 25; Lynn Yeh/Shutterstock.com, 25; CCTV Video News Agency/YouTube.com, 26; jayesh chitre/YouTube.com, 27; Oliver Nicholls/YouTube.com, 27; Chichimaru/Shutterstock.com, 28; Pitsanu Kraichana/Shutterstock.com, 29; Jon Davison/Alamy, 29

About the Cover
Window cleaners dangle from a high-rise building.

Access free, up-to-date content on this topic plus a full digital version of this book. Scan the QR code on page 31 or use your school's login at 12StoryLibrary.com.

Table of Contents

Window Washers Have a Long History 4

Window Washers Deal with Harsh Wind Conditions 6

Window Washers Enjoy Working Outdoors 8

Window Washers Must be Mentally Alert 10

People Look Through High-Rise Windows 12

Window Washers Have Mentors 14

Window Washers Need Special Training 16

Some Window Washers Compete in
Speed-Cleaning Contests 18

Window Washers Earn More with Experience 20

Window Washers Need Special Equipment 22

New Buildings Are Designed with
Window Washers in Mind 24

High-Rise Window Washers Won't Be
Replaced by Robots 26

More Daring and Dangerous Jobs 28

Glossary 30

Read More 31

Index 32

About the Author 32

Window Washers Have a Long History

Chicago's first skyscraper was the Home Insurance Company building, 1884.

and steel. It would be fireproof and tall. In 1884, Jenney's design became the first skyscraper.

Soon, other tall buildings went up in Chicago and New York City. All of the designs

In 1871, the Great Chicago fire destroyed more than 17,000 wooden buildings. Then an engineer named William Le Baron Jenney designed a new way of building. He used iron

Rockefeller Center in New York City.

Window cleaners rely on safety belts.

1936
Year the modern squeegee was invented

- The first window washers used heavy squeegees to clean.
- An Italian immigrant named Ettore Steccone developed a new design.
- His design is still used today.

included a lot of windows. An immigrant from Poland saw an opportunity. He organized a group of window washers.

At first, window washers had to stand on ledges outside the windows. They hung onto the window frames with their fingers. Then in the early 1900s, they began using leather safety belts. The belts had straps that attached to two bolts. The bolts were installed in the bricks around each window.

WASHERS FROM AROUND THE WORLD

Most of the first window washers were from Poland. Later washers included immigrants from Ireland, Ukraine, and Italy. In the 21st century, many high-rise window washers come from South America.

Window Washers Deal with Harsh Wind Conditions

Platforms help keep window washers safe on high buildings.

Buildings are considered tall if they are 14 or more stories high. But many buildings go even higher. Window washers clean all the windows on these tall buildings.

One of the most dangerous parts of the job is dealing with wind.

High winds tossed window washers in Edmonton, Canada.

25

Top wind speed in miles per hour (40 km/h) for washers to stay on the platform

- In October 2019, two window washers were working on the Stantec Tower in Edmonton, Canada.
- Strong winds caused their platform to crash into the building four times.
- One worker fell off the platform and dangled from his harness. Firefighters rescued him from the platform.

Wind can cause the washer's platform or basket to swing. It can blow the ropes around the corner of the building. The platform may even crash into the building. Even a mild wind of 15 miles per hour (24 km/h) can cause it to sway.

THE TALLEST BUILDING IN THE WORLD

The Burj Khalifa is a skyscraper in Dubai. It was completed in 2010. It has 163 floors and is 2,716 feet (828 m) tall. But the Burj Khalifa may not keep its title for long. New, taller buildings are already under construction.

Window Washers Enjoy Working Outdoors

The boatswain chair is a temporary platform designed for one window cleaner.

Many people who become window washers don't like working in offices. They don't want to be in a closed workspace. They enjoy being outside where every day is different. They also enjoy the views from up high.

Many window washers like the peaceful atmosphere, too. They like being alone or with a partner on the side of a skyscraper. They are far from the noise of the streets. They may talk or just work in silence.

Like many other outdoor jobs, window washers sometimes have to deal with nature. For example, window washers

Many window washers enjoy the solitude of working high above the city.

often run into spiders. The spiders get on their clothes or in their hair. Sometimes the window washers are attacked by yellow jackets.

Window washers also deal with birds. In Chicago, falcons build their nests high on the buildings. When window washers come, the birds attack them to protect their nests. Sometimes the window washers have to postpone the job until the baby birds have grown enough to fly away.

Falcons and other birds can be a problem for window washers.

33°

Lowest temperature in degrees Fahrenheit (0°C) in which window washers can work

- Window washers work in all kinds of weather.
- They work in very hot and cold temperatures.
- They often begin the workday just after sunrise.

Window Washers Must be Mentally Alert

High-rise window washers need to stay focused high above the ground.

High-rise window washers often work in difficult conditions. They are hundreds of feet above the ground on a suspended platform. To stay safe, they must always know what is going on around them. They must be able to stay focused and think quickly when problems come up.

This would not be a good job for someone with acrophobia, a fear of heights. But fear is still part of the job because they are up so high. It reminds them to be careful. Otherwise, accidents are more likely to occur.

A window washer must think a lot about safety.

Even then, accidents can happen. In August 2019, a window washer was working on a skyscraper in Chicago. When he was on the 53rd floor, one of his safety ropes snapped. He was left dangling in the air. The Chicago fire department had to pull him up approximately 80 feet (24 m) to the roof and safety.

Window washers dangled 69 stories above the ground in the new World Trade Center in 2014.

88
Number of window washing accidents in the US over a 15-year period

- The Occupational Safety and Health Administration put together the report.
- The report included accidents at homes as well as skyscrapers.
- Sixty-two of the people involved in the accidents died.

5

People Look Through High-Rise Windows

Window washers see some surprising things in their work.

When window washers work, they can see everything happening inside the rooms. Sometimes they are washing the windows of office buildings. They see people working

or playing games on the computer. They can look in on business meetings. Sometimes they see famous people. Sometimes the washers look in on apartments. They see people's messy bedrooms. One window washer saw a person's dog having puppies.

2
Number of times each year window washers dress up in costume at Children's Hospital of Pittsburgh

- Window washers have been dressing up in the spring and for Halloween since 2012.
- One of the directors in the hospital saw a newspaper photo. It was a window washer dressed as Spider Man in London.
- The office manager at the window cleaning company saw the same photo. They started a new tradition.

Many window washers enjoy cleaning children's hospital windows. They wave at the children and make them smile. Sometimes the window washers even dress up. Window washers across the US dress up as superheroes, such as Spider Man and Captain America. They've dressed up as Batman and the Flash. During the Christmas season, some dress up as the Grinch or Santa Claus.

THINK ABOUT IT
What are some things you can do to make someone smile?

6

Window Washers Have Mentors

A mentor is a person who helps guide someone in their education or career. Many high-rise window washers have mentors. Some are family members or friends. Some are other window washers they meet on the job.

Some people become window washers because it's the family business. Their grandfather, father, or brother may already be a window washer. They may even own the company. Some have friends who help get them started.

Newbie window washers learn by watching how the veterans do the job.

High-rise window washers must take training courses. But they also learn a lot from their mentors. The mentors have had many experiences on the job. They share what they have learned. In this way, they can help others avoid mistakes. They can teach them how to become successful.

THINK ABOUT IT

Do you have a mentor? Is there a family member or teacher who has helped you?

1986
Year the Chelsea Window Cleaning company was established in New York

- Robert Hanlon used to work in real estate. But he wanted to be a window washer.
- His father-in-law started a company with just a bucket and some tools.
- Hanlon learned about the business from his father-in-law. Now he's the owner of the company.

Window Washers Need Special Training

Window washers rely on platforms, harnesses, and ropes high above the ground. Some window washers compare it to rock climbing. They need to know how to handle the equipment. They need to know how to stay safe.

Many people think window washing is easy. But the workers must be highly skilled. In the US, window washers train to become certified. Some of the training is done on the job while the window washer is working. The training focuses on how

Safety must come first when working high in the sky.

Safety in numbers may be one reason window washers formed the IWCA.

1989
Year a group of window washers formed a professional organization in Lubbock, Texas

- The window washers created the International Window Cleaning Association (IWCA).
- The IWCA promotes safety and education among window washers.
- IWCA also offers certification programs.

to clean the windows. It also focuses on safety. Washers learn how to use the safety equipment properly.

SAFETY ROPES

Rope access refers to a system of support that uses ropes instead of platforms. One rope supports the workers while a second rope protects them from falling. Window washers aren't required to be trained in rope access. But the training has many benefits. Rope access can be easier, faster, and safer to use than other types of equipment.

Window washers' lives depend on strong ropes.

Some Window Washers Compete in Speed-Cleaning Contests

Window washers take speed-cleaning contests very seriously.

Every year, the International Window Cleaning Association hosts a convention. One of the events is a window-cleaning speed contest. IWCA members and their employees who attend the convention can enter the contest.

Competitors have to clean three 45-square-inch (.029 sq m) windows.

They are given a squeegee, soap, water, and a towel. They can't use their own supplies. The contest is timed by two people. An expert referee scores the work. A half-second is added for each smear, streak, or water spot left on the windows.

18

The IWCA also sponsors two other contests at the convention. One involves windows of different heights. The other is a team competition.

THE WORLD CUP

2019 was the first year for the Window Cleaning World Cup Competition. The Competition was held in London, England. Jeremiah Hickey took first place. His final time was 17.02 seconds. This included 11.02 seconds of washing and 6 seconds for imperfections.

5

Number of times Jeremiah Hickey won the speed-cleaning contest

- Jeremiah Hickey from California won the 2019 contest.
- He started his window cleaning company in 1998.
- The prize includes recognition at the AWARDS Banquet, a championship belt, and free registration to the next convention.

Hickey in the first annual Window Cleaning World Cup in 2019.

Window Washers Earn More with Experience

Window washers earn good money.

One San Francisco company pays its window washers between $17 and $22 an hour. In New York, the buildings are higher. So are the risks the window washers take. A window washer in New York can earn $20 to $35 per hour.

As window washers gain experience, they can earn more money. Their company may give them a raise. They may find a new company to work for with higher pay. They may even start their own business. In 2001, Anthony Natoli decided to

Window washers who are just starting out can earn approximately $15 to $25 per hour. The amount depends on the company they work for. It also depends on where they are located.

become a window washer. He had already worked at jobs that required climbing. But now he wanted to be independent. He started his own window cleaning company in New York.

$20.50

Top wage per hour for many window washers in Chicago in 2018

- In June 2019, high-rise window washers went on strike.
- They stopped working until they could get a new contract with their companies.
- After four weeks, a deal was reached. The window washers could now make $26.00 per hour.

Window Washers Need Special Equipment

permanently fixed to the top of the building. A platform that can carry several washers is suspended from the boom. A carriage is more modern. It is also mounted on the roof. It can rotate from left to right.

Pulleys, ropes, and harnesses are part of the everyday window washing equipment.

Window washers start on the roof. They can move down the skyscraper in several ways. A boom, or long pole, is roof. The washers sit on bosun's chairs. This chair is usually a piece of wood with straps through it, like the seat of a swing.

Window washers need several tools. A soft-bristle brush helps loosen debris. A squeegee cleans the glass. The squeegee has rubber blades that scrape water and dirt off of the window. A mop catches extra water. Buckets hold the water, cleaner, and tools.

Strong hoists and sturdy ropes are required to work safely.

Some window washers rappel down the building. They wear a harness that goes over the shoulders and around the waist. Ropes attach the harness to anchors on the

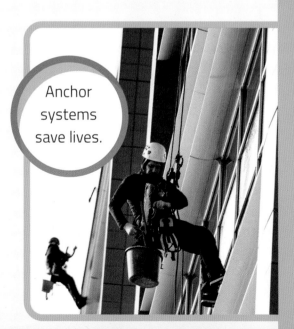

Anchor systems save lives.

5,000
Top weight in pounds (2,268 kg) an anchor system must be able to support

- A portable davit is one of the cheapest ways to move down a building.
- A davit is like a small, moveable crane.
- The rope goes from the davit's metal arm to the window washer.

New Buildings Are Designed with Window Washers in Mind

The unique design of Amazon Spheres in Seattle Washington.

In the past, office buildings had glass windows set in concrete or stone. But as technology improved, glass became stronger. Glass buildings are becoming more and more common. Workers want offices with natural light. Companies want pleasant environments with nice views.

Many of these buildings have unusual designs. Instead of straight sides, some have curving or twisting walls. Others have more than one setback. Architects and

$3 million

Cost of the machine used to clean the windows of the Hearst Tower in New York in 2005

- The architect of the Hearst Tower planned a building shaped like a jewel.
- Engineers had to come up with a new way to wash the windows.
- It took three years to design and build the machine.

builders must figure out how the windows will be cleaned.

THE TOP OF THE TOWER

At night, the top of the Salesforce Tower in San Francisco lights up. Images of dancers move across it. LED lights on rods create the images. The rods stick off the side of the building. Window washers told the engineering team the rods would break when they cleaned the top. The team had to come up with a way to make the rods flexible.

The Salesforce Tower in San Francisco was designed with window washers in mind.

salesforce

High-Rise Window Washers Won't Be Replaced by Robots

Robot window cleaners have limited uses and sometimes the quality is missing.

Some companies are creating robots to wash the windows. That way, people won't be in danger of falling. But many window washers would lose their jobs. And people enjoy seeing them work in the cities.

Some robotic engineers think the window washers would just have different jobs. They believe the washers are the most qualified to control the robots. They could oversee the robots from the ground.

Robots have mostly been used on buildings that are 10 stories high or less. But the buildings have to be made of glass. Other surfaces can mess up the robots. Another problem with the robots is the quality of the work. Often the robots don't clean well. They can't get into the corners the way people can. People have to come back and clean again.

THINK ABOUT IT

If you could program a robot to take your place doing something, what would it be?

19

Age of Oliver Nicholls when he built a robot to wash skyscraper windows

- Nicholls created the robot when he was in the 12th grade in Sydney, Australia.
- His robot is controlled by a computer program.
- Nicholls believes his robot can withstand winds up to 28 miles per hour (45 km/h).

Oliver Nicholls put together his robot window washer in his garage.

More Daring and Dangerous Jobs

Tower Climber

Tower climbers climb and inspect cell phone towers. They often have to climb 200 to 500 feet (60 to 150 m) high. Much of their work involves maintaining the towers. They change out lines, antennas, and light bulbs.

Line Installer and Repairer

Line installers and repairers install or fix electrical power systems and telephone wires. They often work far off the ground with high-voltage electricity. Along with working regular hours, they may also work nights, weekends, and holidays when needed.

Wind Turbine Technician

A wind turbine is a machine that changes wind energy into electricity. Wind turbine technicians install, repair, and maintain these turbines. Sometimes they work underground. Other times they work on top of the turbine, often more than 200 feet (61 m) off the ground.

Glossary

anchor system
A method for securing something to a building so it doesn't fall.

debris
Loose items such as leaves, twigs, or other pieces of material.

falcon
A bird of prey that can dive at 200 miles per hour (322 kph) to catch other birds.

independent
Not controlled by other people or things, or not depending on someone else for a job.

immigrant
A person who whomoves to a foreign country to live permanently.

LED light
A light-emitting diode is a device that produces light using less electricity.

natural light
The light from the sun, compared to artificial light from light bulbs.

rappel
To go down a vertical surface, such as the side of a building, using a rope.

setback
A step-like design in a high-rise building to allow sunlight to reach the lower floors and streets.

skyscraper
A tall building of at least 40 stories, or about 400 feet (120 m), containing offices or apartments.

strike
To refuse to work until an employer agrees to higher wages or better conditions.

suspended
Attached to something and hanging down.

Read More

Finger, Brad. *13 Skyscrapers Children Should Know.* New York, NY: Random House Prestel Publishing, 2016.

Newland, Sonya. *Extraordinary Skyscrapers: The Science of How and Why They Were Built.* North Mankato, MN: Capstone Press, 2018.

Wolny, Philip. *21st Century Skyscrapers.* New York, NY: Enslow Publishers, 2018.

Visit 12StoryLibrary.com

Scan the code or use your school's login at **12StoryLibrary.com** for recent updates about this topic and a full digital version of this book. Enjoy free access to:

- Digital ebook
- Breaking news updates
- Live content feeds
- Videos, interactive maps, and graphics
- Additional web resources

Note to educators: Visit 12StoryLibrary.com/register to sign up for free premium website access. Enjoy live content plus a full digital version of every 12-Story Library book you own for every student at your school.

Index

accidents, 11
acrophobia, 10
alertness, 10–11
anchor systems, 23

building design, 24–25

Children's Hospital, 13
contests, 18–19

dressing up, 13

environment, 8–9
equipment, 16–17, 22–23

Hickey, Jeremiah, 19
history, 4–5

International Window
    Cleaning Association
    (IWCA), 17, 18–19

line installer and
    repairer, 29
looking through windows,
    12–13

mentors, 14–15

Nicholls, Oliver, 27

outdoor work, 8–9

rappeling, 23
robots, 26–27

squeegees, 5

tallest building, 7
temperatures, 9
tower climber, 28
training, 15, 16–17

wages, 20–21
wind turbine technician, 29
winds, 6–7
worldwide window
    washers, 5

About the Author

Samantha S. Bell has written more than 125 nonfiction books for children. She also teaches art and creative writing to children and adults. She lives in the Carolinas with her family and too many cats.